Push·up Pops

Push·up Pops

Courtney Dial Whitmore

Photographs by Kyle Dreier

GIBBS SMITH
TO ENRICH AND INSPIRE HUMANKIND

First Edition

16 15 14 13 12   5 4 3 2

Text © 2012 Courtney Dial Whitmore
Photographs © 2012 Kyle Dreier

Published by
Gibbs Smith
P.O. Box 667
Layton, Utah 84041

1.800.835.4993 orders
www.gibbs-smith.com
www.pizzazzerie.com

Designed by Jennifer Barry Design, Fairfax, California
Printed and bound in China
Gibbs Smith books are printed on either recycled, 100% post-consumer waste, FSC-certified papers or on paper produced from sustainable PEFC-certified forest/controlled wood source. Learn more at www.pefc.org.

Library of Congress Cataloging-in-Publication Data

Whitmore, Courtney Dial.
  Push-up pops / Courtney Dial Whitmore ; photographs by Kyle Dreier.
— 1st ed.
     p. cm.
  ISBN 978-1-4236-2531-5
1. Ice pops. I. Title.
  TX795.W64 2012
  641.86'3—dc23
                    2011041628

To my mother, for her enthusiasm, creative talent, and passion for celebrating life's moments.

Contents

Acknowledgments

Big thanks to Jennifer Adams and the Gibbs Smith team for believing in me and helping me make this book a reality! Thank you to Kyle Dreier for your hard work, long hours, and creative expertise. Thank you also to Caroline Brewer and Rory White for putting the finishing touches on every shot. Thank you to David and Laura for your advice and remote kitchen expertise. Thank you to Katie Whitmore for capturing me at my best. Thank you to my taste-testers: Chris Whitmore, Tyler and Nicole Rhoden, and Henry. Lastly, thank you to the dedicated readers and fans of Pizzazzerie.com for your daily excitement.

Celebrating and hosting parties has been a love of mine since I set up my first tea party as a little girl. Entertaining friends and family brings together those we love to enjoy great food and even sweeter company. I am so excited to share this collection of party recipes for your own special occasions. Push-up pops are perfect for themed children's birthday parties, spooky Halloween parties, summer picnics, Christmas parties, Easter gatherings, Valentine's day parties, tea parties, baby showers, bridal showers, or for a push-up pop baking swap!

Tips and Techniques for Push-up Pops

You might remember frozen push-up pops from your childhood, and now these sweet treats are back as the latest party trend.

There are no rules with push-up pops! From frozen novelties to cakes and pies, almost any dessert recipe can be transformed to fit in these little dishwasher-safe containers (for a list of places to buy them, see Resources, page 92). In this book, you'll find a collection of fabulous sweet recipes for push-up pops. Following are some tools and equipment that will make creating your push-up pops as easy as can be.

Jelly Roll Baking Pan

A jelly roll pan is similar to a cookie sheet but with raised sides. Recipes in this book were developed using an 11 x 16-inch jelly roll pan. For cakes, cookies, and bar recipes, simply spread your batter or dough out to fill the jelly roll pan. There's no need for a cookie cutter. Simply flip your push-up pop container over and use the container itself to cut and push out circles. Flip it back over to fill the push-up pop with your baked goods.

Frosting Tips

Many recipes in this book call for piping frosting, whipped topping, or various fillings. If you don't have a frosting dispenser or a pastry bag with tips, simply place your frosting or filling in a large, plastic ziplock bag. Fold down sides of the bag when filling it to avoid making a mess. Fold the sides up and cut a small hole in one corner of the bag. You are now ready to pipe and swirl your filling or frosting into the push-up pop molds. To pipe a pretty swirl, lift up in a circular motion as you squeeze the filling out.

Layering Tool

To help press down layers of a recipe (for example: cake, frosting, graham cracker crumbs), I created an easy tool from the "push-up" part of the push-up pop mold itself. Use scissors to trim the raised edge of the "push-up" piece so you are left with a flat

round base on a stick that can be inserted into the push-up pop container to push down each layer as you build the filled push-up pop.

Displaying Your Push-Up Pops

To display your sweet treats, simply push the handle of your filled push-up pop mold down into floral foam placed in a vase or bowl. Hosting a rustic themed party? Place floral foam in wooden crates and cover with natural-colored crinkle paper. Throwing a tropical luau? Cover floral foam with shaved coconut.

Acrylic and plastic push-up pop stands can be found online (see Resources, page 92) or you can easily make your own by drilling small holes in wood. Then paint the wood to fit your party theme! Raise the wooden frames on pedestals to make room for the handles underneath.

Following are some helpful hints for baking.

Measurements

$\frac{1}{8}$ teaspoon = a pinch or dash

3 teaspoons = 1 tablespoon

2 tablespoons = 1 fluid ounce = $\frac{1}{8}$ cup

4 tablespoons = $\frac{1}{4}$ cup

1 pound = 16 ounces

1 cup = 8 fluid ounces = 16 tablespoons

1 pint = 2 cups

1 quart = 2 pints = 4 cups

1 gallon = 4 quarts = 16 cups

Baking Measurements

$\frac{1}{2}$ cup butter = 1 stick = 8 tablespoons

4 cups flour = 1 pound

2 cups sugar = 1 pound

1 pound brown sugar = $2\frac{2}{3}$ cups

1 pound powdered sugar = $3\frac{1}{2}$ cups

1 square chocolate = 1 ounce

1 cup chocolate chips = 6 ounces

1 cup whipping cream = 2 cups whipped

1 lemon = $\frac{1}{4}$ cup lemon juice

1 orange = $\frac{1}{3}$ cup orange juice

$\frac{1}{2}$ cup all-purpose flour and $\frac{1}{2}$ cup cornstarch
   = 1 cup cake flour

Cake Push-up Pops

Strawberry Shortcake

Host a strawberry shortcake party with this sweet treat. Serve up a variety of strawberry goodies (chocolate-dipped strawberries, strawberry daiquiris, strawberry mousse) and encourage guests to bring their favorite strawberry recipe to share!

¾ cup butter, divided

1 box pound cake mix

4 eggs, room temperature, divided

1 (8-ounce) package cream cheese

1 (16-ounce) box powdered sugar

1 teaspoon vanilla extract

2 pints strawberries

whipped cream topping

Preheat oven to 350 degrees F. Melt ½ cup of the butter and combine with pound cake mix and 2 eggs. Mix with an electric mixer until ingredients are well blended. Spread into a greased jelly roll pan. Set aside.

Melt the remaining ¼ cup butter. Soften the cream cheese in a microwave-safe bowl. Beat the cream cheese, remaining 2 eggs, powdered sugar, melted butter, and vanilla with an electric mixer until fluffy, 3 to 5 minutes. Pour over cake mixture in pan, sealing the edges. Bake for 45 minutes or until golden brown. Cool and cut into circles using the open end of a push-up pop mold.

Slice the strawberries or cut into small pieces. Start layering a push-pop mold with a circle of cake followed by a dollop of whipped cream topping. Add a layer of strawberries. Repeat layers. Garnish the top with strawberries. Chill until ready to serve.

Makes 12 push-up pops

Rainbow Cupcake Party

You can change the color of the cake and frosting in this recipe to match your party or holiday occasion. Turn this into a glittery princess dessert with pink cake and a sprinkle of edible glitter. Or try these combinations: For Halloween, use orange, yellow, and white. For Christmas, use red and green. For Valentine's day, use red and white. For St. Patrick's Day, use green and white. For baby showers, use pastel blue and pastel pink.

1 package white cake mix

food coloring

Buttercream Frosting
½ cup butter, softened

3 cups powdered sugar

¼ cup milk

½ teaspoon vanilla extract

¼ teaspoon almond extract

½ cup shortening

Preheat oven to 350 degrees F. Prepare the cake according to the directions on the box. Divide batter into as many separate small bowls as colors of cake you want. Place 3 to 4 drops of food coloring in each bowl of batter and stir until colored. Pour colored batter into a greased mini muffin pan. Bake for 10 to 12 minutes. Let cool.

For buttercream frosting, cream butter and powdered sugar until well mixed using an electric mixer. Add the milk, vanilla, almond extract, and shortening and beat until a frosting consistency is achieved, 3 to 5 minutes.

Line up layers of cake in push-up pop mold as desired. Top with a swirl of frosting.

Makes 24 push-up pops

Dreamy Chocoholic

Host a chocolate party! Serve up a variety of sweet chocolate treats including a tasting bar with different varieties of chocolate such as bittersweet, semisweet, milk, white, and so on. Or just serve these push-up pops as a sweet ending to any delicious meal.

1 package chocolate cake mix

1 small package instant chocolate pudding

1 (8-ounce) container sour cream

½ cup vegetable oil

½ cup warm water

4 eggs, room temperature

1½ cups semisweet chocolate chips

Chocolate Frosting

3 cups powdered sugar

½ cup butter

½ cup shortening

¼ cup milk

½ teaspoon vanilla extract

1 cup semisweet chocolate chips, melted

Preheat oven to 350 degrees F. Combine the cake mix, pudding mix, sour cream, oil, water, and eggs. Beat with an electric mixer for 5 minutes. Stir in the chocolate chips. Pour batter into a greased jelly roll pan and bake for 20 minutes. Cool and cut into circles using the open end of a push-up pop mold.

For chocolate frosting, combine the powdered sugar, butter, and shortening and beat until blended. Add the milk, vanilla, and melted chocolate and continue beating until fluffy, 2 to 3 minutes.

Place a layer of chocolate cake in the bottom of a push-up pop mold. Top with a swirl of chocolate frosting. Repeat until full. End with swirl of chocolate frosting.

Makes 34 push-up pops

Gingerbread Jingle

Decorate push-up pops by hot gluing a large jingle bell to the top of the container and wrapping holiday ribbon around the push-up pop.

⅓ cup butter, melted

⅓ cup light brown sugar

⅓ cup sugar

½ cup molasses

2 eggs, room temperature

½ cup milk

1 (8-ounce) container sour cream

1 ¾ cups all-purpose flour

1 teaspoon baking soda

¼ teaspoon salt

2 teaspoons cinnamon, plus more
    for garnish

¼ teaspoon nutmeg

1 teaspoon ground ginger

¼ teaspoon ground cloves

Cream Cheese Frosting

1 (8-ounce) package cream cheese,
    room temperature

½ cup butter, softened

1 teaspoon vanilla extract

1 (16-ounce) box powdered sugar

Preheat oven to 350 degrees F. Mix together the melted butter, sugars, molasses, eggs, milk, and sour cream.

In a separate mixing bowl, stir together flour, baking soda, salt, cinnamon, nutmeg, ginger, and cloves. Gradually add dry ingredients to wet ingredients, mixing well. Bake for 20 minutes in a greased jelly roll pan. Cool slightly and cut into circles using the open end of a push-up pop mold.

To make cream cheese frosting, beat cream cheese, butter, and vanilla with an electric mixer until well blended. Add powdered sugar, 1 cup at a time, and continue to blend well.

Place one gingerbread circle in the bottom of a push-up pop mold and top with a swirl of cream cheese frosting. Then add another gingerbread circle and end with a swirl of frosting. Garnish with a dash of cinnamon.

Makes 17 push-up pops

Limoncello Delights

Limoncello is an Italian lemon liqueur made using lemon zest. Its rich, lemony flavor is perfect for outdoor summer entertaining. Send these little limoncello delights home with friends as a sweet party favor.

4 eggs, room temperature

1 package yellow cake mix

1 small package instant lemon pudding

⅓ cup lemon juice

⅓ cup vegetable oil

⅓ cup Limoncello

Zesty Orange Frosting

½ cup butter, softened

1 (16-ounce) box powdered sugar

¼ cup frozen orange juice concentrate, thawed and undiluted

1 teaspoon orange zest

1 teaspoon Limoncello

Preheat oven to 350 degrees F. Using an electric mixer, beat eggs until thick and lemon colored. Add the cake mix, pudding mix, lemon juice, oil, and Limoncello; beat on medium speed for 10 minutes. Pour into a greased jelly roll pan and smooth batter evenly in pan. Bake for 20 minutes. Cool and cut into circles using the open end of a push-up pop mold.

For zesty orange frosting, beat the butter, powdered sugar, and thawed orange juice concentrate with an electric mixer until well blended. Add the orange zest and Limoncello and continue beating until fluffy.

Assemble the push-up pops by putting a dab of frosting in the bottom of a push-up pop mold and then a Limoncello cake. Top with orange frosting. Repeat layers until full. End with a swirl of orange frosting.

Makes 20 push-up pops

Christmas Coconut Cake

This coconut cake is especially wonderful at Christmas with its deep red color and white frosting. Wrap a Christmas bow around the push-up pop and adorn with a miniature ornament to decorate.

1 box white cake mix

2 (1-ounce) bottles red food coloring

Coconut Frosting

1 (8-ounce) package cream cheese, room
   temperature

1 (16-ounce) box powdered sugar

2 tablespoons milk

1 teaspoon vanilla extract

2 cups sweetened flaked coconut

candy sprinkles

Preheat oven to 350 degrees F. Prepare the cake according to the directions on the box. Add both bottles of red food coloring and beat until well mixed. Bake in a greased jelly roll pan for 30 minutes. Cool and cut into circles using the open end of a push-up pop mold.

For coconut frosting, beat cream cheese and powdered sugar with an electric mixer until blended. Add milk and vanilla. Add a little more milk, if needed, to reach frosting consistency. Stir in sweetened coconut.

Assemble push-up pops by placing one red cake circle in the bottom of a push-up pop mold and topping with a swirl of coconut frosting. Repeat layers of cake and frosting until full. Garnish with candy sprinkles.

Makes 20 push-up pops

Tiramisu

Host an Italian-style cocktail party with mini foods like bruschetta, caprese skewers (cherry tomato, basil leaf, and mozzarella ball drizzled with balsamic dressing), bize-size dishes of tortellini and lasagna, and, of course, tiramisu push-up pops.

16 ounces mascarpone cheese

1 cup heavy cream

½ cup sugar

½ cup unsweetened cocoa powder, divided

2 tablespoons coffee liqueur

6 ounces espresso or strong coffee

1 purchased pound cake

chocolate-covered espresso beans or shaved chocolate, for garnish

In the bowl of an electric mixer fitted with a whisk attachment, beat together mascarpone cheese, cream, sugar, 2 tablespoons unsweetened cocoa powder, and coffee liqueur. Beat until stiff peaks form.

Slice pound cake into 1-inch-thick slices and cut into circles using the open end of a push-up pop mold. Assemble push-up pops by placing one cake circle into the bottom of a push-up pop mold. Drizzle with 1 tablespoon espresso or coffee. Top with a layer of mascarpone filling. Sprinkle with a dash of unsweetened cocoa. Repeat layers until full. Garnish top with unsweetened cocoa, shaved chocolate, or a chocolate-covered espresso bean. Refrigerate until ready to serve.

Makes 8 push-up pops

Pineapple Upside-Down Cake

The next time you have a poolside party, why not make it a Hawaiian luau and serve Pineapple Upside-Down Cake push-up pops? Greet guests with a colorful lei and a push-up pop as they enter the party. Or try freezing piña coladas in push-up pop molds for a cool summer treat.

1 box white cake mix

1 (20-ounce) can pineapple tidbits

1 cup brown sugar

4 tablespoons butter, melted

pineapple slices, for garnish

maraschino cherries, for garnish

Preheat oven to 350 degrees F. Prepare the cake batter according to the directions on the box. Drain the pineapple tidbits and combine with the brown sugar and butter. Pour the pineapple mixture into a greased jelly roll pan. On top of this mixture, carefully pour the cake batter to cover. Bake for 30 minutes. Cool for 5 minutes and then flip the pan over to expose the pineapple side. Let cool again before assembling.

Use the open end of a push-up pop mold to cut out circles from the cake. Place one cake circle in the bottom of a push-up pop mold, pineapple side up. Then place another cake circle on top of that one. Fill push-up pop to the top with cake circles and garnish with a slice of pineapple and a maraschino cherry.

Makes 11 push-up pops

Wedding Cake

Serve wedding cake push-up pops to guests at wedding showers and receptions. Decorate the container with a sticker of the couples' monogram, a strand of beaded pearl trimming, or a mini tulle veil.

1 cup butter

3 cups sugar

1 cup sour cream

1 cup milk

5 eggs, room temperature

3 cups flour

1 teaspoon salt

1 tablespoon almond extract

½ teaspoon lemon extract

Almond Buttercream Frosting

4 ounces cream cheese

½ cup butter

3 ½ cups powdered sugar

1 tablespoon milk

1 tablespoon almond extract

½ teaspoon lemon extract

edible candy pearls

Preheat oven to 350 degrees F. In the bowl of an electric mixer, beat the butter and sugar until well blended. Add the sour cream and milk and continue beating. Next add the eggs, one at a time, beating after each addition. Add the flour, salt, and almond and lemon extracts and beat until well combined. Bake in a greased jelly roll pan for 35 to 40 minutes. Cool and cut into circles using the open end of a push-up pop mold.

For the almond buttercream frosting, soften the cream cheese and butter in the microwave, 20 to 30 seconds. Add the powdered sugar and beat with an electric mixer. Next add the milk, almond extract, and lemon extract and beat until fluffy.

Assemble the push-up pops by starting with a little icing in the bottom of a push-up pop mold. Add a layer of cake and repeat layers until push-up pop is full. Top with a swirl of almond buttercream frosting and decorate with edible candy pearls.

Makes 20 push-up pops

Tuxedo Cake

Use ribbon to make a mini bow tie and hot glue it to your push-up pop for a cute decoration on this black-and-white treat. I'll be serving these cuties at my own wedding.

4 eggs, room temperature

1 box dark chocolate fudge cake mix

1 small package instant chocolate pudding

1/3 cup vegetable oil

1 cup sour cream

White Chocolate Buttercream Frosting

1 cup butter, softened

3 cups powdered sugar

6 ounces white chocolate, melted

3 tablespoons half-and-half

1 teaspoon lemon juice

1/2 teaspoon vanilla extract

1/2 teaspoon salt

Preheat oven to 350 degrees F. Beat eggs until thick and light yellow. Add cake mix, pudding mix, oil, and sour cream and continue beating for 10 minutes. Pour into a greased jelly roll pan and bake for 30 to 35 minutes. Cool and cut into circles using the open end of a push-up pop mold.

For the white chocolate buttercream frosting, combine butter and powdered sugar and beat with an electric mixer until fluffy. Pour in white chocolate, half-and-half, lemon juice, vanilla, and salt. Beat for 2 to 3 minutes or until well combined.

Fill a large plastic ziplock bag or frosting dispenser with white chocolate buttercream frosting. Layer one round of chocolate cake in the bottom of a push-up pop container. Top with a swirl of frosting. Layer with another round of cake followed by another swirl of frosting.

Makes 20 push-up pops

Pie Push·up Pops

Key Lime Pie

∙∙∙

Transport to the islands with this tart and creamy key lime pie push-up pop. Perfect for a backyard summer party.

5 large egg yolks

1 (14-ounce) can sweetened condensed milk

1 tablespoon lime zest

½ cup fresh lime juice

1½ cups graham cracker crumbs

2 tablespoons sugar

4 tablespoons butter, melted

whipped cream topping

lime slices, for garnish

Preheat oven to 325 degrees F. Combine the egg yolks, condensed milk, lime zest, and lime juice in a heavy saucepan. Cook over low heat, stirring constantly until the mixture thickens or boils, about 10 minutes. Pour into a greased pie pan. Bake for 25 minutes. Let cool.

For the crust, combine the graham cracker crumbs, sugar, and butter. Mix until well blended and set aside. Place cooled key lime pie mixture into a large plastic ziplock bag and snip off corner.

To assemble push-up pops, start by pressing 1 to 2 tablespoons of crumb mixture into the bottom of the push-up pop. Pipe a swirl of key lime pie filling onto the graham cracker layer. Repeat until full. Top with whipped cream topping and garnish with a slice of lime. Refrigerate until ready to serve.

Makes 10 push-up pops

Tailgate Apple Crunch

· ·

The fall brings football, tailgating, and lots of fresh apple treats.

Apple Filling

1½ cups vegetable oil

2 cups sugar

3 eggs, room temperature

3 cups all-purpose flour

1 teaspoon salt

1 teaspoon baking soda

1 teaspoon ground nutmeg

1 teaspoon ground cinnamon

3 tablespoons vanilla extract

3 cups diced Granny Smith apples

1 cup pecans, chopped

½ cup butter

1 cup brown sugar

1 teaspoon vanilla extract

½ cup milk

Pecan Crunch

2 cups pecan halves

½ teaspoon salt

½ cup brown sugar

¼ cup butter, melted

Preheat oven to 325 degrees F. Beat the oil, sugar, and eggs with an electric mixer until well blended. Add the dry ingredients. Stir in vanilla, apples, and pecans. Pour batter into a greased jelly roll pan. Bake for 24 to 28 minutes or until lightly golden and cooked through. Let cool.

Mix butter, brown sugar, vanilla, and milk in a saucepan. Bring to a rolling boil and pour over the cooled cake. Let cool completely and then chill in the refrigerator for at least 1 hour.

Stir together ingredients for pecan crunch until nuts are well coated. Place in a single layer on a baking sheet lined with parchment paper. Bake at 350 degrees F for 12 to 15 minutes, stirring several times. Cool.

Use the open end of a push-up pop to cut out circles in the iced cake. Place one cake circle in the bottom of a push-up pop mold and top with 1 to 2 tablespoons of pecan crunch. Repeat layers until full. Garnish with whipped cream, if desired.

Makes 17 push-up pops

Pumpkin Pie

· ·

Start your Thanksgiving celebration off right with pumpkin pie push-up pops. For the kids who love a fun crafts project, set out a variety of paper, markers, stickers, and fall-themed craft supplies. Encourage them to decorate the push-up pop containers with fall leaves, Thanksgiving scenes, and pumpkins.

1 (15-ounce) can pumpkin

1 (14-ounce) can sweetened condensed milk

3 egg yolks

½ cup firmly packed brown sugar

½ teaspoon ground ginger

½ teaspoon ground cloves

½ teaspoon ground cinnamon

2 ½ cups ground gingersnaps

4 tablespoons butter, melted

1 refrigerated piecrust

1 drop yellow food coloring

2 tablespoons powdered sugar

1 teaspoon water

whipped cream topping

cinnamon, for garnish

Preheat oven to 350 degrees F. In the bowl of an electric mixer, combine the pumpkin, condensed milk, and egg yolks and beat until smooth. Add the sugar and spices and stir until well blended. Pour into a greased pie pan. Bake for 50 to 55 minutes or until firm. Let cool. Place filling in a large plastic ziplock bag and snip off corner.

Put ground gingersnaps in a medium bowl and pour in melted butter. Stir until combined.

Use leaf-shaped mini cookie cutters or a knife to create small leaves in the refrigerated piecrust. Use knife to draw leaf veins. Place the leaves on a baking sheet and bake at 450 degrees F for 5 minutes. Let cool.

Make icing by combining powdered sugar, water, and yellow food coloring. Using a spoon, drizzle the icing on the baked leaves and let dry.

To assemble push-up pops, place 1 to 2 tablespoons of gingersnap mixture in the bottom of a push-up pop mold. Swirl pumpkin pie filling on top of gingersnap layer. Continue layering until full. Garnish filled push-up pops with a swirl of whipped cream topping and decorate with an iced piecrust leaf. Complete with a dash of cinnamon on top.

Makes 10 push-up pops

Oreo Cheesecake

· ·

Oreo cheesecake is a perfect treat for baby showers, wedding showers, and birthday celebrations. For a birthday party, buy colorful birthday candles to embellish your cheesecake. Your birthday guest will love blowing out the candle on her push-up pop treat.

2 cups Oreo cookie crumbs

4 tablespoons butter, melted

1 (24-ounce) container cheesecake filling

mini Oreo cookies, or more cookie crumbs, for garnish

Combine Oreo cookie crumbs and melted butter and stir until mixed. Put 1 to 2 tablespoons of Oreo crumb mixture in the bottom of a push-up pop mold.

Place cheesecake filling in a large plastic ziplock bag and snip off corner. Pipe a swirl of cheesecake filling on top of Oreo crumb layer. Repeat layers until full. Top with a swirl of cheesecake filling. Garnish each push-up pop with mini Oreo cookies or more cookie crumbs. Refrigerate until ready to serve.

Makes 14 push-up pops

Snickers Caramel Pie

. . . .

An ooey, gooey treat for all Snickers lovers, this caramel pie is a crowd-pleaser. Perfect for all sorts of themed soirees—pirates, circus or carnival, robots, and rockets!

1 (8-ounce) package cream cheese, room temperature

½ cup crunchy peanut butter

1½ cups powdered sugar

4 regular Snickers candy bars, chopped

1 (8-ounce) container frozen whipped topping, thawed

3 cups chocolate wafer cookie crumbs

4 tablespoons butter, melted

caramel sauce

sliced Snickers candy bars, for garnish

Beat cream cheese, peanut butter, and powdered sugar in the bowl of an electric mixer until smooth. Stir in chopped Snickers bars and then fold in whipped topping until creamy and blended. Refrigerate for 1 hour. Pour into a large plastic ziplock bag and snip off corner.

Combine chocolate cookie crumbs and melted butter. Put 1 to 2 tablespoons of cookie crumb mixture into the bottom of a push-up pop mold. Pipe a layer of Snickers filling on top of cookie crumb mixture. Drizzle with caramel sauce. Repeat until full. End with a layer of Snickers filling and garnish with caramel sauce and Snickers bar slices. Refrigerate until ready to serve.

Makes 10 push-up pops

Banana Cream Pie

Southern to its core, the banana cream pie is fitting for gender-neutral baby showers such as a Rubber Ducky theme.

1 small package instant banana cream pudding

1½ cups milk

4 ounces cream cheese, room temperature

4 ounces sour cream

3 ripe bananas

mini vanilla wafer cookies

whipped topping

Combine pudding mix, milk, cream cheese, and sour cream in the bowl of an electric mixer and beat until smooth. Refrigerate for 1 hour. Place chilled banana cream filling in a large plastic ziplock bag and snip off corner. Slice bananas in thin slices.

To assemble the push-up pops, layer 3 mini vanilla wafers in the bottom of a push-up pop mold. Pipe banana cream filling on top of vanilla wafer layer. Add a layer of sliced bananas. Repeat until full. Garnish with whipped topping and a mini vanilla wafer.

Makes 15 push-up pops

Minty Chocolate Crème Pie

The green and chocolate colors on this sweet treat make it absolutely fantastic for everything from monster-themed bashes to Easter parties. Adorn the push-up pop filling with a marshmallow bunny for Easter or decorate the push-up pop mold with a cute monster sticker and ribbon for Halloween.

1 (8-ounce) container frozen whipped topping, thawed

1 cup sweetened condensed milk

4 ounces cream cheese, room temperature

¼ cup crème de menthe

¼ teaspoon lemon extract

¼ teaspoon peppermint extract

8 drops green food coloring

1 package mint crème chocolate graham cookies

In a large bowl, combine the whipped topping, sweetened condensed milk, cream cheese, crème de menthe, and lemon and peppermint extracts. Beat ingredients until blended; add green food coloring. Continue beating until thoroughly mixed. Refrigerate for 1 hour. Spoon filling into a large plastic ziplock bag and snip off corner.

Assemble the minty chocolate crème pie push-up pops by placing one mint crème cookie in the bottom of a push-up pop mold. Pipe in 1 tablespoon of the creamy mint mixture. Repeat layers until full. Garnish with a cookie.

Makes 10 push-up pops

Zesty Lemon Pie

....

Serve up this cool and refreshing pie for all sorts of occasions. I think it's fabulous for backyard luncheons, book club refreshments, or birthday parties.

1 (8-ounce) container frozen whipped topping, thawed

1 (14-ounce) can sweetened condensed milk

1 (8-ounce) package cream cheese, room temperature

1 tablespoon lemon zest

½ cup fresh lemon juice

¼ teaspoon almond extract

½ cup pecans, chopped

1 cup sweetened coconut flakes (optional)

1½ cups vanilla wafer crumbs

lemon zest

Combine whipped topping, sweetened condensed milk, and cream cheese and stir until well blended. Add the lemon zest, lemon juice, almond extract, pecans, and coconut, if using; stir again. Refrigerate for 3 to 4 hours.

Make crust by mixing the vanilla wafer crumbs and butter. Press 1 tablespoon of the crust mixture in the bottom of a push-up pop mold. Add 2 tablespoons of lemon filling. Repeat layers until full. Return to the refrigerator. When ready to serve, garnish with lemon zest.

Makes 10 push-up pops

Frozen Push·up Pops

Watermelon Surprise

Make this treat for the Fourth of July or any other summer party. Serve alongside fresh watermelon slices for the perfect dessert.

1½ quarts lime sherbet, softened

1½ quarts vanilla ice cream, softened

1½ quarts strawberry sorbet, softened

1 (12-ounce) package semisweet
   chocolate chips

Spoon 2 to 3 tablespoons of lime sherbet in the bottom of a push-up pop mold. Make the next layer using 1 tablespoon of vanilla ice cream. Next, fill mold to the top with strawberry sorbet. Press chocolate chips on top of the strawberry sorbet to resemble watermelon seeds. Freeze until ready to serve.

Makes 40 push-up pops

Frozen Strawberry Lemonade

The possibilities are endless for this fruit Popsicle. Swap out strawberries for fresh raspberries or blueberries. Swap out lemonade for grapefruit juice for extra tartness or use your favorite fruit juice instead. Just keep the measurements the same for the fruit to juice ratio and use variations to your heart's delight.

4 cups strawberries, cored and quartered

2 cups lemonade

½ cup sugar

Place strawberries, lemonade, and sugar in a blender and puree until smooth. Pour strawberry puree into push-up pop molds. Add tops and place the handles in a block of floral foam to ensure push-up pops stay upright. Place in freezer overnight.

Makes 10 push-up pops

Frozen Lime Margarita

Host a Mexican fiesta and greet guests at the door with these frozen lime margaritas, rimmed in salt. Try a variety of flavors by adding in frozen strawberries, mangos, or other fruit. For a fun presentation, try rimming the edges of the push-up pop molds in salt or sugar before pouring in the lime mixture.

5 cups ice

6 ounces limeade concentrate, thawed and undiluted

6 ounces tequila

¼ cup triple sec

2 tablespoons lime juice

1 tablespoon lemon juice

lime slices, for garnish

Puree ice, limeade concentrate, tequila, triple sec, and fruit juices in a blender until smooth. Fill push-up pop molds with frozen margarita mixture and serve, or place in freezer if preparing in advance. Garnish with a slice of lime.

Makes 10 push-up pops

Pink Champagne Freeze

Elegant and refreshing, these pink champagne freezes are the perfect treat for baby showers, bridal showers, and other special occasions. So toast to friends with a champagne push-up pop. Cheers!

1 quart lemon sorbet, softened

½ pint raspberry sorbet, softened

2 cups champagne

1 teaspoon lemon zest

1 pint fresh raspberries

Combine the softened lemon and raspberry sorbets in a medium mixing bowl. Add the champagne and lemon zest. Stir until well blended and place in freezer for at least 1 hour. After it is frozen, spoon champagne freeze into the push-up pop molds. Place the tops on and place molds in the freezer until ready to serve. Garnish with fresh raspberries before serving.

Makes 12 push-up pops

Frozen Peach Bellini

Greet guests at wedding receptions or cocktail parties with this refreshing frozen treat. The mild and sweet peach flavor and touch of sparkling wine make it elegant for hot summer nights.

3 cups Prosecco or sparkling wine

1 cup peach schnapps

3 cups sliced frozen peaches

1 cup ice

Combine all ingredients in a blender and puree until smooth. Pour into push-up pop molds and place in the freezer for 1 hour or until ready to serve.

Makes 15 push-up pops

Peppermint Candy Cane

Tips for this fun holiday recipe: (1) Egg whites will yield more volume if at room temperature when beaten. (2) Meringues should be made on a day when humidity is low or they will not be crisp. (3) Use parchment paper when baking meringues to protect them from any oil residue that might be on your pans.

2 egg whites, room temperature

⅔ cup sugar

½ teaspoon vanilla extract

½ teaspoon almond extract

½ teaspoon cream of tartar

red food coloring

½ gallon peppermint ice cream

peppermint candy sticks

Preheat oven to 375 degrees F. Beat the egg whites until stiff peaks form. Gradually add the sugar, vanilla and almond extracts, and cream of tartar. Add two to three drops of red food coloring and continue beating until the mixture is very stiff.

Line a cookie sheet with parchment paper. Using the end of a push-up pop mold as a guide, trace circles on the parchment paper. Pipe the meringue batter on the circles, making them slightly smaller than the traced circles. Place cookie sheet in preheated oven and *turn off* the oven. Leave meringues in oven overnight. Next morning, remove cookie sheet from oven and store the meringues in an airtight container until ready to use.

To assemble push-up pops, fill a push-up pop mold with 1 to 2 tablespoons of peppermint ice cream and top with a meringue cookie. Repeat layers until full. Freeze until ready to serve. Garnish with peppermint candy sticks.

Makes 20 push-up pops

Mocha Madness

Ring in the New Year with this Mocha Madness. Serve it instead of serving coffee at your New Year's Eve party.

Hot Fudge Sauce

3 (1-ounce) squares unsweetened chocolate

1 cup sugar

1 small can evaporated milk

¼ cup butter

1 teaspoon vanilla extract

1 package Oreo cookies

⅓ cup butter, melted

1 pint coffee ice cream, softened

1 can chocolate hazelnut pirouette cookies

To make hot fudge sauce, mix the chocolate, sugar, and evaporated milk in a double boiler and heat until melted and smooth. Stir in the butter and vanilla until blended and heated through.

Place 28 Oreo cookies in a ziplock bag. Seal bag and crush cookies using a rolling pin until they are in very small pieces. Mix the cookie pieces with the melted butter.

To assemble push-up pops, layer 1 to 2 tablespoons of cookie pieces into the bottom of a push-up pop mold. Add 1 tablespoon of coffee ice cream. Top that with 1 tablespoon of fudge sauce. Repeat layers until full. Freeze push-up pops until ready to serve.

When ready to serve, remove the tops and let soften a few minutes. Cut pirouette cookies in half and stick two half-cookie sticks in the top of each push-up pop and serve. Refrigerate leftover fudge sauce for use with other ice cream treats.

Makes 12 push-up pops

Banana Split

Set up a banana split push-up pop bar with sliced bananas, a variety of ice cream flavors, and lots of mini candies. Guests young and old will enjoy making this old-fashioned dessert.

3 bananas

1 pint vanilla ice cream

1 cup hot fudge sauce (see Mocha Madness, page 68)

candy sprinkles

maraschino cherries

Slice bananas 1-inch thick. Place 1 banana slice into the bottom of a push-up pop mold. Layer with 2 tablespoons of vanilla ice cream. Next add a drizzle of hot fudge sauce. Repeat layers until full. Garnish each with candy sprinkles and a cherry.

Makes 12 push-up pops

Dreamsicle Daiquiri

Celebrating an engagement or anniversary? This makes the perfect treat. It's also fantastic for poolside parties and retro-themed events.

1½ **pints orange sorbet**

¾ **cup half-and-half**

¾ **cup orange juice**

6 **ounces light rum**

3 **ounces triple sec**

5 **cups ice**

Blend together orange sorbet, half-and-half, orange juice, light rum, triple sec, and ice in a blender until smooth. Pour in push-up pop molds and seal with tops. Freeze until ready to serve.

Makes 10 push-up pops

Cookies, Candy, and More

Chocolate Chip Cookie

Turn this classic cookie into a sweet push-up pop treat! Enjoy with a glass of ice-cold milk. Have a chocolate chip cookie party and ask guests to bring printed copies of their favorite cookie recipe to share.

2 ¼ cups all-purpose flour

1 teaspoon baking soda

1 teaspoon salt

1 cup butter, room temperature

¾ cup sugar

¾ cup packed brown sugar

2 teaspoons vanilla extract

2 large eggs

3 cups semisweet chocolate chips

1 (16-ounce) container vanilla frosting

chocolate chips, for layering

Preheat oven to 375 degrees F. Combine flour, baking soda, and salt; set aside. Cream together butter, sugars, and vanilla until well blended. Add eggs, one at a time, beating well after each addition. Gradually pour dry ingredients into wet ingredients until mixed well. Stir in chocolate chips.

Spread batter onto a greased jelly roll pan and bake for 15 to 17 minutes or until slightly golden. Let cool slightly and use an empty push-up pop mold to cut out circles.

Assemble push-up pops by putting a little vanilla frosting in the bottom of a push-up pop mold. Sprinkle on a few chocolate chips. Add a cookie circle. Repeat layers until full, ending with frosting topped with a few chocolate chips.

Makes 12 push-up pops

Campfire S'mores

Pitch a tent and host a camping party. You can have it in a canyon, campground, park, or your own backyard! Send guests home with these s'more push-up pops as a sweet favor.

4 tablespoons butter, melted

3 cups graham cracker crumbs

1 (16-ounce) container marshmallow fluff

1 (16-ounce) container chocolate frosting

4 regular-sized chocolate bars

mini marshmallows, for garnish

Combine melted butter and graham cracker crumbs and set aside. Place the marshmallow fluff in a large plastic ziplock bag and snip off corner. Place 1 to 2 tablespoons graham cracker crumbs in the bottom of a push-up pop mold. Top with a swirl of marshmallow fluff, about 1 to 2 tablespoons. Add a layer of chocolate frosting. Repeat layers, ending with a square of chocolate bar and mini marshmallows on top.

Variation: Mix it up by adding in a layer of peanut butter or chocolate hazelnut spread.

Makes 17 push-up pops

Peanut Butter Lovers

The favorite of photographer Kyle Dreier, this push-up pop can be enjoyed for just about any occasion. It's especially fitting for a circus-themed fete, so hit the craft store for carnival- and circus-themed stickers, ribbon, and adornments.

1 cup butter, softened

1 cup sugar

½ cup brown sugar

2 eggs, room temperature

1½ cups peanut butter

1¾ cups all-purpose flour

1 teaspoon vanilla extract

1 teaspoon salt

1 teaspoon baking soda

Peanut Butter Frosting

1 (8-ounce) package cream cheese, room temperature

¼ cup butter, softened

1 cup peanut butter

1 teaspoon vanilla extract

1 (16-ounce) box powdered sugar

½ teaspoon salt

miniature peanut butter cups, for garnish

In a large mixing bowl, beat together butter and sugars until well blended. Add the eggs and peanut butter and continue beating until combined. Add the flour, vanilla, salt, and baking soda. Beat until combined. Cover the bowl and refrigerate for at least 1 hour. Remove and spread into a greased jelly roll pan. Bake at 375 degrees F for 15 minutes. Let cool and cut into circles with the open end of a push-up pop mold.

For peanut butter frosting, combine the cream cheese, butter, and peanut butter and beat until well blended. Add the vanilla, powdered sugar, and salt and continue beating until fluffy, about 2 to 3 minutes. Place frosting in a large plastic ziplock bag and snip off corner.

Assemble the push-up pops by putting one peanut butter cookie circle into the bottom of a push-up pop mold. Swirl a layer of frosting on the cookie. Repeat layers until full, ending with a swirl of frosting. Cut mini peanut butter cups in half and place on top of push-up pops to garnish.

Makes 15 push-up pops

Valentine's Truffle Treat

Celebrate this lovers' holiday by serving up sweets for your sweetie! These truffle treats are perfect as gifts for your girlfriends too. Pink heart decorations, Valentine's ribbon, and a sweet note are all you need to add a little pizzazz to the push-up pop containers.

5 (1-ounce) squares semisweet chocolate

3 (1-ounce) squares white chocolate

1/3 cup butter

2 tablespoons whipping cream

1 cup powdered sugar

1/4 teaspoon vanilla extract

1/4 teaspoon almond extract

1/4 teaspoon salt

1 (8-ounce) bag Heath English Toffee Bits

1 (16-ounce) container chocolate frosting (optional)

Melt the chocolates and butter in a heavy saucepan over medium to low heat, stirring constantly. Remove from the stove and stir in the cream, powdered sugar, vanilla and almond extracts, and salt. Cool slightly (15 to 20 minutes). This makes a chocolate truffle mixture.

Place Heath English Toffee Bits in a shallow dish. Shape chocolate truffle mixture into 1-inch balls and roll them in toffee bits. Store truffles in an airtight container in the refrigerator.

To make push-up pops, layer 3 truffles in each push-up pop container. You can add a dollop of chocolate frosting between each truffle, if desired.

Makes 8 push-up pops

Birthday Brownie Sundae

Add fun to any occasion with these mini brownie sundaes. Coordinate your party colors and decorate push-up pops with patterned ribbon secured with hot glue. Head to your fabric store for dozens of designs and prints to create tablecloths. Decorate in red and aqua for a whimsical and retro touch to your party.

8 (1-ounce) squares unsweetened chocolate

1 cup butter

5 eggs, room temperature

3 cups sugar

1 tablespoon vanilla extract

1 teaspoon almond extract

1½ cups all-purpose flour

1 (6-ounce) package semisweet chocolate chips

1 quart vanilla ice cream or whipped cream

candy sprinkles

maraschino cherries

Preheat oven to 375 degrees F. Melt chocolate and butter in a heavy saucepan over low heat, stirring often. Cool slightly. Beat eggs, sugar, vanilla extract, and almond extract in a large mixing bowl until combined, about 2 to 3 minutes. Add the melted chocolate mixture and beat on low speed. Next add the flour and beat just to blend. Stir in the chocolate chips. Pour into a greased jelly roll pan and bake for 20 to 25 minutes. Cool in pan.

Use the open end of an empty push-up pop mold to cut circles out of brownies. Stack 2 brownie circles in each push pop. Just before serving, top with a scoop of vanilla ice cream or whipped cream. Garnish each with sprinkles and a cherry.

Makes 17 push-up pops

Mini Cinnamon Buns

. . . .

Host a weekend brunch and serve up these sweet push-up pops along with mini pancakes and parfait push-up pops. Include a build-your-own mimosa bar!

1 can Pillsbury seamless crescent dough

1 tablespoon ground cinnamon

2 tablespoons brown sugar

2 tablespoons white sugar

¼ cup butter, melted

Icing

½ cup powdered sugar

2 tablespoons water or milk

⅛ teaspoon vanilla extract

Preheat oven to 375 degrees F. Unroll the dough and cut into 4 equal sections. Combine the cinnamon and sugars, mixing well. Brush one-fourth of the melted butter over one section of dough all the way to the edges. Sprinkle one-fourth of the cinnamon-sugar mixture over the top. Starting with the wide side, roll up the dough as tightly as possible; pinch the ends to hold in shape when baking. Repeat for the three remaining dough sections. Using a pizza cutter or sharp knife, slice the rolled up dough into circles about ⅓-inch thick and place circles in a greased mini muffin pan. Bake in preheated oven for about 8 minutes.

For icing, combine the powdered sugar, water or milk, and vanilla and stir until well blended. Drizzle icing over mini cinnamon buns. Stack 3 to 4 mini cinnamon buns in each push-up pop mold.

Makes 8 push-up pops

Sweet 'n' Salty Caramel Cookie

When all the little ghouls and goblins show up at your house for your Halloween party, treat them with a Sweet 'n' Salty push-up pop.

¾ cup salted butter, softened

1 cup light brown sugar

½ cup sugar

2 large eggs

2 teaspoons vanilla extract

2 cups all-purpose flour

1 teaspoon baking soda

½ teaspoon salt

1 (12-ounce) package semisweet chocolate chips

3 cups mini pretzels, coarsely chopped

Salted Caramel Frosting

1 cup salted butter, softened

1 (16-ounce) box powdered sugar

¼ cup caramel sauce

1 teaspoon sea salt

mini pretzels, for garnish

Preheat oven to 350 degrees F. Beat butter and sugars in the bowl of an electric mixer until fluffy. Add eggs, one at a time, and mix well. Add vanilla. Combine flour, baking soda, and salt in a separate bowl. Slowly add dry ingredients to wet ingredients until combined. Stir in chocolate chips and pretzel bits. Spread batter in a greased jelly roll pan and bake for 25 to 30 minutes or until golden brown. Let cool slightly. Use the open end of an empty push-up pop mold to cut out circles from baked cookie.

For salted caramel frosting, beat butter and sugar in the bowl of an electric mixer until fluffy. Add caramel sauce and salt. Beat for 1 minute. Place frosting in a large plastic ziplock bag and snip off corner.

To assemble the push-up pops, layer one cookie circle in the bottom of a push-up pop mold. Pipe a swirl of salted caramel frosting on top of cookie. Repeat layers. Garnish with a mini pretzel.

Makes 14 push-up pops

Coconut Blueberry Parfait

Fill your ice cooler full of coconut blueberry parfaits for a "very berry" sweet picnic. Head to your nearest park or lake and enjoy! You may want more than one of these light and refreshing desserts, so be sure to have extras!

3 cups fresh blueberries

24 ounces vanilla yogurt

1 box purchased coconut cookies

Using a sharp knife, chop up the cookies into small pieces. Place 2 teaspoons of yogurt in the bottom of a push-up pop mold and sprinkle some blueberries on top. Add a layer of cookie pieces. Repeat layers until full. End with yogurt and top with blueberries. Refrigerate until ready to serve.

Makes 14 push-up pops

Resources

Push-Up Pops

For small orders, 5+
    shop.pizzazzerie.com

For medium orders, 12+
    lagunawholesale.com
    pushpopcontainers.com
    thebakerskitchen.net
    thesugardiva.com

For bulk orders, 100+
    bakedeco.com
    culinarydirect.com
    martellatousa.com

Candies and Sprinkles

    bakeitpretty.com
    sweetbakingsupply.com
    thebakerskitchen.net

Baking Pans and Frosting Dispenser

    bakedeco.com
    thebakerskitchen.net
    wilton.com

Party Ideas and Baking Recipes

    amyatlas.com
    bakerella.com
    hostesswiththemostess.com
    marthastewart.com
    pizzazzerie.com

Push-Up Pop Display Holders

    culinarydirect.com
    cupcake-stand.com
    jbprince.com
    martellatousa.com
    pastrychef.com
    pushpopcontainers.com
    shop.pizzazzerie.com
    thebakerskitchen.net

Index

Metric Conversion Chart

Volume Measurements		Weight Measurements		Temperature Conversion	
U.S.	*Metric*	*U.S.*	*Metric*	*Fahrenheit*	*Celsius*
1 teaspoon	5 ml	½ ounce	15 g	250	120
1 tablespoon	15 ml	1 ounce	30 g	300	150
¼ cup	60 ml	3 ounces	90 g	325	160
⅓ cup	75 ml	4 ounces	115 g	350	180
½ cup	125 ml	8 ounces	225 g	375	190
⅔ cup	150 ml	12 ounces	350 g	400	200
¾ cup	175 ml	1 pound	450 g	425	220
1 cup	250 ml	2¼ pounds	1 kg	450	230